chronicle

mick yates

Clare Songbirds Publishing House Poetry Series
ISBN 978-1-957221-05-2
Clare Songbirds Publishing House
chronicle © 2022 Mick Yates

Printed in the United States of America
FIRST EDITION

140 Cottage Street
Auburn, New York 13021
www.claresongbirdspub.com

Contents

All of the poems
in this short collection
were written during the global
Coronavirus pandemic
of 2020/21
they are a record of my own experiences
during those dark and strange times

sensory deprivation

in the middle of the coronavirus lockdown
i awaken one morning in a silent world
to find myself in yet another place of isolation
one that deprives me of my hearing
and deepens my understanding
of the concept of solitary confinement
a sudden and serious ear infection
has rendered me more aware than ever
of the fragility and uncertainty of life
and the frivolity of the fates
that gamble with our destiny
with a subtle sleight of hand
when they shuffle the card deck of our lives
meanwhile i feel suspended in time and space
like an astronaut on a mission to another planet
with no lifeline to tether me to the mother ship
should the antibiotics work as i hope they will
then i shall eventually return to our world
hopefully a little wiser than before i left
a with a greater appreciation also
of what life has yet to offer me
in this beautiful if misguided planet of ours

magic

there is still much magic
in this world of ours
if you only have eyes to see
and wonder in your heart
it is not locked away secretly in treasure chests
buried in chambers deep underground
it is there for all to discover
do not seek it out though
rely on your instinct
trust your senses to find the way
and when you do finally arrive there
you will surely know the place
for it is holy and unchangeable
it has existed forever
and will continue to do so
while there are people in this world
who still believe in such things
for many wonderful dreams are born there
and without dreams we are lost

clouds

on a day such as this in september
the sky changes from one minute to the next
the wind blows forcefully
moving clouds like chess pieces
across the distant horizon
the sun appears then disappears
there is heat from the sun sometimes
and then there is the cold shadow
a reminder that winter is on its way
and that nothing is permanent in this world
everything is transient and temporary
passing as swiftly as the clouds today
and as meaningless as some old forgotten song
or the endless ebb and flow of time

stir crazy

days come and days go
they pass by slowly and relentlessly
with the daily routines of life
as waves do on the beach
with the ever changing tides
for how long does it go on though?
weeks then months then years?
the end seems forever out of reach
tears are being shed daily
for those washed up on the shore
the whole world wonders for how much longer?
and for how much more?
until everything returns to normal as it was before
but what is normal anymore?
so many questions still linger on
but yet it still continues
and coronavirus still goes on

questions

do not ask
how long the day will be
or when the sun
will cease to shine
for these are things
best left alone
and to worry about them
is a waste of precious time

me

this poem is about me
the first one i have ever written
that is exclusively about myself
i view the world now through the eyes of a child
even though i am very old in years
these are the toys with which i used to play
they are tarnished and worn with passing time
my wine glass is the cup of a child
when i love it is with an innocent purity
i use words poorly and with no skill
for language is something i have yet to learn
my poems are my emotions laid bare
expressed in words of naïve simplicity
i tell the truth as i perceive it to be
yet i lie to your face sometimes
i am something of a charlatan to be honest
i am much flawed in my own way
yet i am entire and perfectly formed

nimrod

the cat sits
in the fading light of day
waiting for darkness
to hunt for nocturnal prey
he never moves a whisker
still as a statue
silent as a ghost
this is the time he loves most
stalking his prey in the undergrowth
of a nearby house
when the time is right
he strikes like a bolt of lightning
seizing his victim with his taloned paws
ripping its neck with long razor claws
then slowly he devours his captive mouse
leaving me his reluctant witness
to retire upstairs to uneasy sleep
under the brutal blanket of night

stones

an old man skims flat stones
on a bank of the river
as he did many years ago
when he was a young boy
one after the other
time and time again
repeatedly and endlessly
each stone contains a memory
a reminder of what has been lost
with the passing of time
the river carries them swiftly away
as ripples of a life now fading fast
soon to be on its way also
to the estuary and far out to sea

good companions

the fells are my friends
whenever we go walking together
we get on with each other well
even if we both prefer silence
and although our conversation may be sparse
it is still full of significance
the buzzards and the sheep
sometimes eavesdrop as we pass by
sharing intimacies with each other
neither of us cares too much however
for they are notorious gossips
as everyone knows

flotsam

adrift on the wide ocean that is life
rudderless and not knowing
in which direction to paddle anymore
i abandon myself to the prevailing currents
in the hope that they might carry me to the shore
or to some hospitable harbour
where i would be made welcome
and might find a safe haven once more

grief

what can i write about sorrow
that has not been said many times before
by others much more eloquent than me?
maybe i should write
about the loss of something precious
and the hole that it leaves behind
in the fragile fabric of the universe?
if only i could find the right words
i would put them down on paper
but i am far too distraught too fragile
to even consider such a proposition
and too weary to even try
for i fear that what i write
might make me want to cry

memories

now you are gone
everything i see reminds me of you
there are memories lurking everywhere
the books you once read are there
the dresses you left behind
smell of your perfume still
your aura lingers on
all around the house we once shared
there is nowhere for me to escape
from our past life together
i feel trapped here
unable to erase you from my memory
yet afraid sometimes even to try
for fear of disappearing forever
into some deep dark void

poems

tell them simple
tell them straight
write from your heart
not from your head

cloud watching

lie on your back in the sun
with your eyes to the sky
and your body contoured
against the firm form of the fell
relax then tell me what you see
not the type of clouds
their scientific name is irrelevant to me
rather tell me what the clouds
reveal about themselves to you
that is far more important
than their actual nomenclature
what shapes and what animals
what visions and what futures
do they suggest to you?
do you have a dialogue with them yet?
do you understand what i see there?
don't you marvel at their sculptured forms?
or don't you really care?

another day

waking up and getting out of bed
is the first major achievement of the day
usually at six o'clock in the cold black morning
sleep does not come easily these days anyway
mostly interspersed with strange vivid dreams
and regularly recurring nightmares
of feeling trapped and isolated in life
within a stark bleak cell of the mind
regular daily routines dominate the horizon
get up, wash, have breakfast
check the television news for instructions
then go shopping for food and other essentials
wearing a facemask for safe anonymity
read a book, play my favourite music
have lunch, read some more
go for a long walk if the weather is fine
read a book, watch the clock as time moves slowly onward
prepare the evening meal next, washed down with gin and wine
read some more, watch television, play some more music and snooze
feed the cats one last time, watch the latest news
then retire to bed once more to sleep fitfully and snore
through the inevitable nightmares that haunt our lives
in these desolate lockdown times

feline lockdown

the cats are moping around these days
like a pair of lovesick teenagers
getting up late in the day
always wanting endless food and drink
never exercising outside the house
staying in bed late sleeping constantly
or listening to music all day on the radio
when spoken to they might grunt a miaow
and skulk back to their baskets
sulky, moody and hormonally dysfunctional

towel dance

it is windy outside today
and two towels are dancing
in the swirling air outside my window
they shimmy and sway on the washing line
always in unison always in time
sometimes a passionate tango
then a waltz maybe sensual and serene
and as they drift across the open-air ballroom
they are as one in their movement
blissful within the fluency of each other
as they dance together eye to eye
against the azure backdrop of the sky
from inside the house i loudly applaud them
and while calling out for an encore
as the judge i give them both ten out of ten
for my considered final score

final reckoning

there have been too many deaths
over the last decade or so for us to endure
these things cast a dark shadow over life
and tend to freeze the soul forever
but then there have been many births also
and many reasons to celebrate life once more
so many grandchildren of ours
to replace the old ones gone forever
although still remembered in our hearts
and in that sense at least
the books have been reconciled
the accounts finally signed off and approved
with this final balance in hand for us both
we should feel well satisfied at last
pleased that though life has taken from us
it has given back to us in many ways
and our personal audit is now finally complete

return to eden

whenever i come back home to cumbria
from the savage cities of the south
my heart always beats faster
my mind expands outwards
as an ever-inflating balloon
so much space in which to dwell
so many possibilities of which to tell
the whole cloistered world outside
so much rugged beauty to shout about
across the wide unforgiving fells
that however bleak you may perceive them to be
tell of time of earth and of longevity
of sadness and of mirth
of death and of rebirth

writing poems

as i approach seventy
the only thing i appear
to be able to do anymore
is to write the very rare occasional poem
and in these twilight days
not even that comes very easily
where is the fluidity?
where is the passion and the emotional power
that i once had when i was younger?
and when those few poems also disappear forever
tell me what is there left for me then
as i approach seventy?

winter solstice

the dark time
of the year is here once again
a time of short days
and of long endless nights
but take hope and fear not
cultivate a positive attitude my friend
for these days will soon end
as from now on the days get longer
as each passing night becomes shorter
until the time will dawn for sure
when the light shall prevail once more

my perfect world

there is an island
in my perfect world
small but perfectly formed
in the middle of a large lake
it is a place where i retreat to sometimes
when the reality of the world i inhabit
overwhelms me and fills me with terror
for a future which i can clearly envisage
it is a place of isolation
where like some saint or hermit
i can exist alone in solitude in silent contemplation
and ponder what might have been
in what once upon a time
was our glorious garden of eden

lockdown

i wonder if the birds
outside our bedroom window
that gather in the tree there
in the early morning
know what is going on?
do they understand
what is happening in our world?
it is fearful and silent
and there are no people
in the streets of our small town
there is no real humanity out there
getting on with the mundane activity
of everyday life anymore
we are all imprisoned behind closed doors
all is silent all is empty
of normal human discourse
it is a ghost town
where the viruses hold sway
hopefully not forever though
i breathe in the cool spring air
on a new morn
and feel glad to be alive
for there will come another day
there will be another dawn

coronavirus

when this has all passed
when this is old news and long forgotten
when we reflect upon it all
let us not remember the isolation
the need to separate ourselves from others
the fear of being with friends
or in the company of strangers
the dread of selfish avarice
the terror of being without food
the futility of such a life
when this is all over
let us embrace all that it is to be human
let us understand that as individuals
we are part of a living community
that we have families and children
that we have friends and neighbours
that the world is a small fragile place
and that life is tenuous in truth
we are here for a reason
and that reason is to embrace others
and to love all of humanity

the past

when you open this door
you are turning the page
to many long-lost memories
some things are best left forgotten
sealed away in boxes forever
that should never be opened again
names that should not be recalled
memories that should not be revisited
except with a certain sadness
and forever tinged with regret
as old love letters yellow with time
so does the past grow brittle
turning to dust as all things do
gently sifting through your fingers

the living flame

falling in love
is like making a fire
a spark some kindling some wood
is all that it takes
to make it burst into life
with the fierce heat of passion
the most sensual of pleasures
and the special intimacy of romance
but the with age and the passing years
the flames can sometimes fade
if they do then begin again once more
add more wood to the dying embers
renew the passion and the living flame
before it all eventually turns to ashes

the estuary

a place where river meets sea
a place of marshland
that smells of life and death
of promise and decay
where water and brine meet
and mingle as they unite
this is where the river
ends its meandering journey
and where the infinity
of the sea absorbs it forever
where all love disappears
becoming what it was
before it ever really existed

Mick Yates lives in the far north of England. He has worked extensively as a playwright and has had more than thirty plays produced at theatres across the country. He has received many awards including an Edinburgh Festival Fringe First and The Benn Levy Award. He has also written for television, most notably for the BBC series **Doctors**. His debut poetry collection **artefacts** won the 2014 Geoff Stevens Memorial Poetry Prize and was published by Indigo Dreams Publishing in 2015. His second collection **kaleidoscope** was published by them in 2017. **the art of conversation** was published by the New York based Clare Songbirds Publishing House in 2018. Another collection **the shapes of passion** was also published by Clare Songbirds Publishing House in 2018 to be followed by **random thoughts from the north** which was published by them in 2019. His next collection **the blue hour** was published by The Hedgehog Poetry Press in 2019. He was longlisted in 2017, 2018 and 2019 for Best Poetry Pamphlet in the prestigious Saboteur Awards and was also a Pushcart Prize nominee in 2018. His pamphlet **poems from egypt** was published by Barley Cottage Publications in 2020 and five other pamphlets **forever in eden , conversing with bees, a river flows through here, from the fells to the sea,** and **bittersweet** were also published by them in 2020.

www.ingramcontent.com/pod-product-compliance
Lightning Source LLC
Chambersburg PA
CBHW020922140626
46545CB00015B/1222